Bring a Thing

by Rachel Russ

illustrated by Aaron Cushley

Tommy was excited. It was Thursday, the best day of the week. That evening, he had Thursday club.

At Thursday club they played games. They also sang songs and made things.

Each week, one child would take in something interesting. They would tell everyone all about it.

This week it was Mabel's turn. She was showing her toy plane. It was silver and shiny. It even had a pilot.

"Thanks, Mabel," said Az, the club leader.

"We meet again on the eighth of June," said Az. "It is Tommy's turn to bring a thing."

Tommy gulped. What could be his thing to bring?

At the weekend, Dad took Tommy to the beach. On the way there, Tommy couldn't stop thinking about bring a thing.

"You are very quiet," said Dad. "Is something the matter?"

"It's my turn to bring a thing," Tommy blurted out.

"That's great!" said Dad.

"Everyone has shown cool toys," Tommy replied. "I feel shy showing mine."

"The toys do not matter. You are kind and funny," said Dad. "That's what matters."

"You will think of something," added Dad. "You're full of great ideas."

Tommy frowned. Was he really full of great ideas?

At the beach, the sky was grey. The sea was still with hardly a ripple.

"Let's skim stones," said Tommy, picking up a pebble.

Suddenly, Tommy spotted a rather odd stone. It had a spiral on it. He picked it up.

“Hey, Dad! What’s this?” asked Tommy.

Dad held it up to get a better look. “It’s a fossil!” he exclaimed. “This is a sea animal from many years in the past.”

Tommy was excited. “Could it be my bring a thing?” he asked.

“As long as you look after it,” replied Dad.

It was Thursday at last. Tommy couldn't wait to show the fossil.

"Tommy, are you able to show something today?" asked Az.

Tommy went to his bag. He lifted out a plastic box.

"What's in the box, Tommy?" asked Maxwell excitedly.

"Let's wait and see," said Az.

"I went to the beach with my dad," Tommy started.

A hush fell around the room.

"That's when I saw it," he said, smiling.

He looked around at everyone. They all wanted to find out what was in the box.

"What did you see?" asked Asma.

Tommy slowly pulled the lid off the box. "I found a fossil," he said proudly.

Everyone wanted to get a better look.

"Thank you, Tommy," said Az. "That was so interesting! I think we could go fossil hunting next Thursday."

At the weekend, Tommy saw Dad again.

“You were right!” Tommy said with delight. “Everyone loved my fossil.”

"See," smiled Dad. "You must trust in yourself. You are full of great ideas."

"I have a great idea now," said Tommy.

"What's that?" asked Dad.

"Let's get chips for tea!" Tommy said, beaming.

Dad grinned. "That's your best idea yet, Tommy."

Look Back

Use the pictures to help you retell the story.

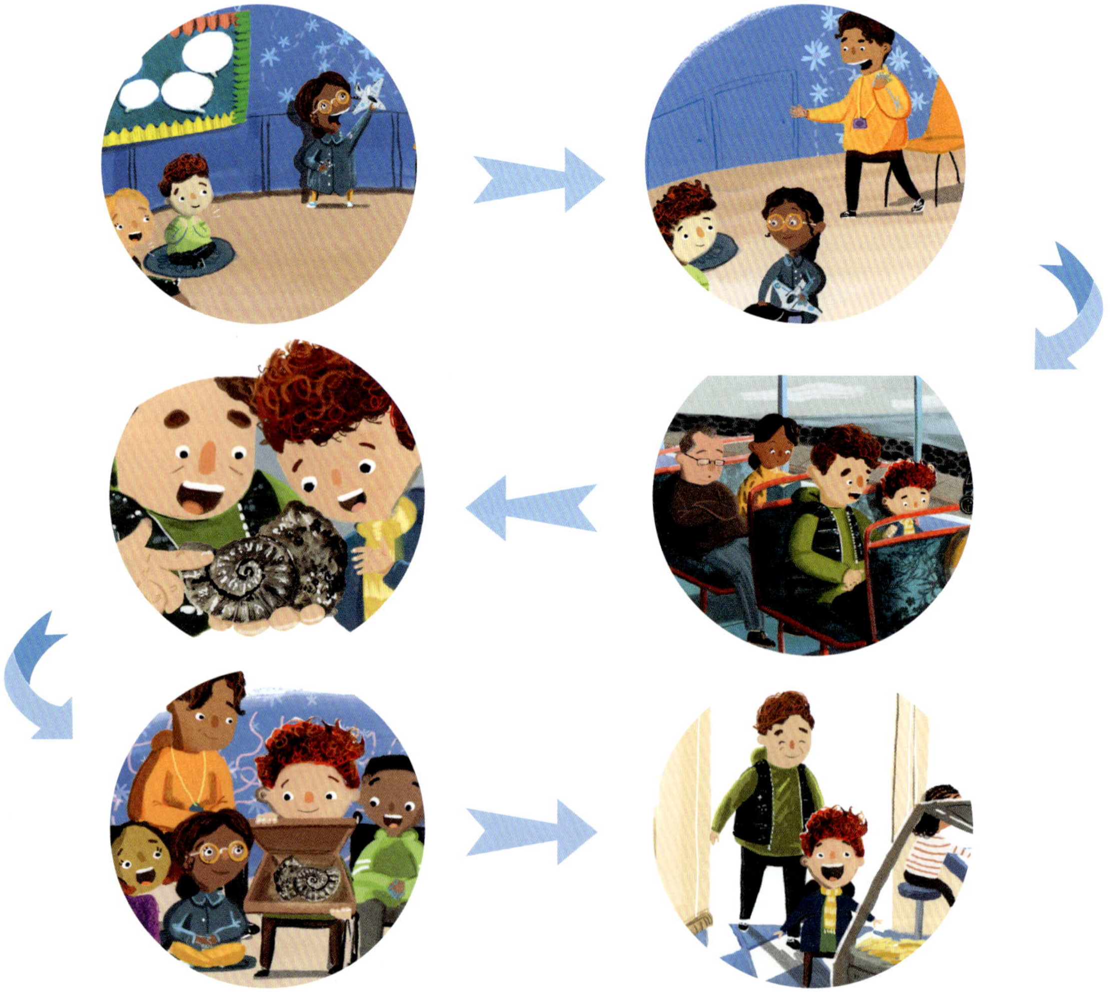

Encourage students to use the pictures to retell the story.